IN AND *OUT* OF BEING **FOOD BLOGGER**

THIS BOOK WILL GUIDE ON EVERYTHING YOU NEED TO
KNOW ABOUT BEING A FOOD BLOGGER.FROM WORKING
ON VIDEOS TO WORKING WITH RESTAURANTS.

I0517908

HUNYAH IRFAN

ISBN: 978-1-968061-38-8

Table of Contents

Introduction

Hi, my name is Hunyah Irfan.

I'm a content creator and food blogger.

I have a background in community development, but I'm a foodie, and I love eating different cuisines and giving my reviews about it.

Background of HunyahTravels

HunyahTravels began in 2019 as a blog written by Hunyah Irfan.

I was 28 at that time in 2019 when I first started my blog.

My written blog didn't last that long.

But I started doing Facebook livestreams in 2020.

By the end of 2020, I started HunyahTravels YouTube Channel, and from there,

HunyahTravels is there for anything food-related, events, and more.

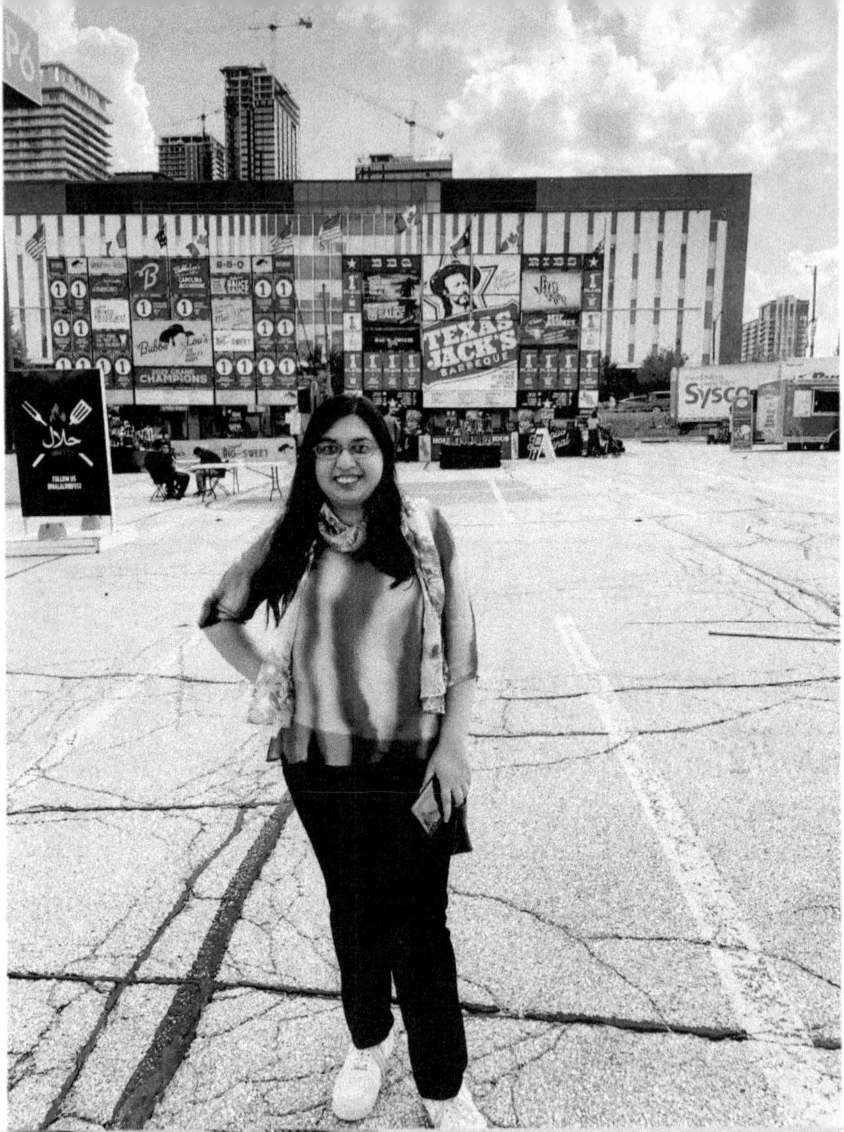

HUNYAH
TRAVELS

Services

Pageant Coaching

 Interviews

HunyahTravels@gmail.com

What Role Do Influencers Have When It Comes to Food Industry

When it comes to the food industry, what is an influencer's role?

1. Promote the brand
2. Promote the menu
3. Collaborate
4. Promote viral trends
5. Connect with the restaurant
6. Increase restaurant reviews
7. Increase social media outreach for the restaurant
8. Travel to different cities to experience different cuisines
9. Share the importance of the dish
10. Promote discounts
11. Affiliate marketing
12. Influencer marketing

How Does
a Food Influencer Work

Food influencer marketing works in a certain format. First, the restaurant or event host shares an ad for food influencers.

Usually, there is a requirement to be a food influencer for a restaurant.

This depends on your social media.

Then, once a food influencer applies to the influencer call, the restaurant discusses the terms of the food influencer's work.

This includes such things, for example:

1. Outreach
2. Instagram stories to share
3. What time to be at the venue
4. What is the restaurant promoting

Then, once the restaurant and influencer start to work on the task.

This is where the food influencer comes in and discusses what is being promoted by the food influencer.

This is:

1. New menu
2. Limited time menu
3. Discount
4. Sale
5. New food line

Now, it is the food influencer who has to try the dishes and give reviews.

This is done with a lot of videos.

Once the food is documented, it is up to the influencer to create and edit the video.

The completed video is then shared on social media.

As a food influencer, promoting the restaurant at the end is important.

You have to subscribe to my channel to try this restaurant.

Rise of Food Tourism Blogging

I don't know when food tourism blogging began. That is because food tourism is on social media. You can see videos, reels, posts, and food tours on YouTube, Facebook, Instagram, and TikTok.

As of 2024, everyone is doing food tour videos. That can be if you are a new YouTuber or an experienced one. Every single person on YouTube has done a food tour. Also, they even reviewed a restaurant.

Everyone has reviewed a food festival.

The reason why my focus is on food tourism. That is because of this, it's a rapid, huge trend.

There are so many different YouTubers who cover food tours.

The only thing that differentiates one YouTuber from another is the style of food tours.

How Do Food YouTubers Differentiate from Each Other?

1. Style of Review
2. Types of venues
3. Types of restaurants
4. Country-based reviews
5. City-based reviews
6. Purpose of the review
7. Types of cuisines
8. Different fast food restaurants

I will discuss food YouTuber methods, tips, and tricks later.

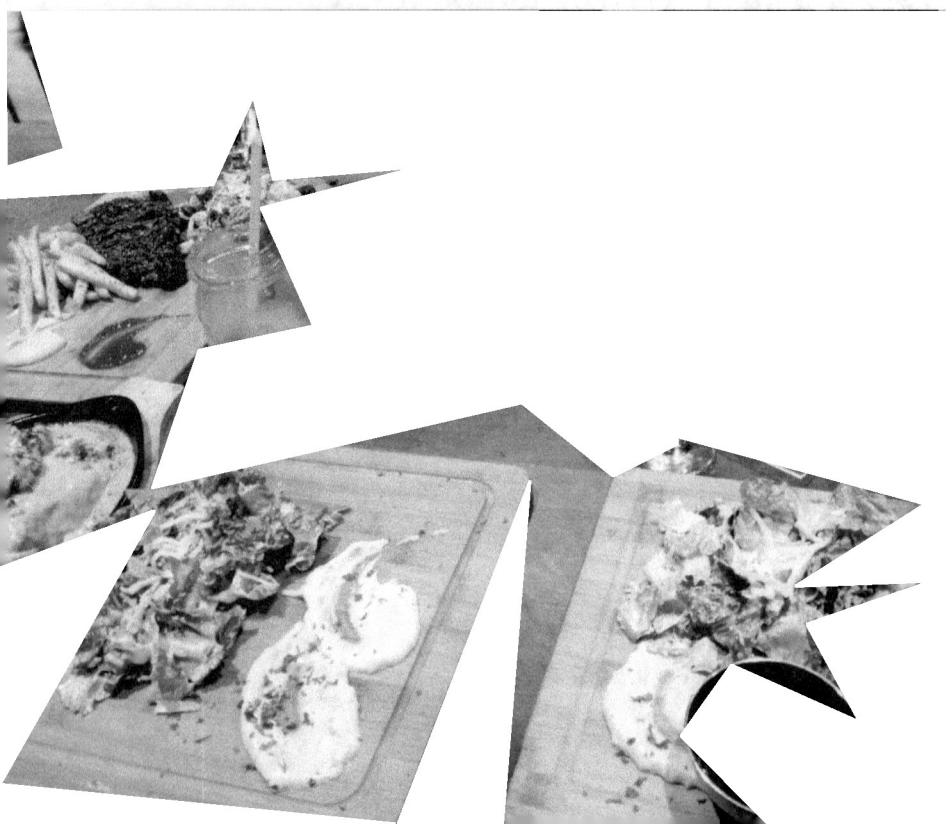

Food Tourism in Canada Is Growing

As a food blogger, I have seen that food tourism is growing in Canada.

Since 2022, the well-known food bloggers have often visited Canada.

However, if you see the videos on YouTube, it's in Toronto where most food bloggers visit when they come to Canada.

Because of TikTok, there is so much growth in food tourism.

There are food festivals every weekend, starting from May of each year.

Then there are halal food festivals for Muslim people.

As a Local Food Blogger, How Is Food Tourism Growing?

As a local food blogger myself, I can say there are new restaurants opening every weekend.

In the Greater Toronto Area, which is known as GTA, there are food plazas everywhere.

The most popular halal food plaza right now is Ridgeway Plaza.

Ridgeway Plaza is located in Erin Mills in Mississauga.

There are about 160 restaurants, according to a video I have seen. Food bloggers are there at Ridgeway Plaza all the time, reviewing new restaurants.

Other places are like Scarborough, Markham, and Brampton, where restaurants are opening up daily.

There are different trends that are coming up every week, thanks to TikTok for bringing the food tourism trends to Canada.

As a food blogger, I can say there is huge growth in food tourism in Canada.

At first, it used to be students going out and eating, trying new restaurants.

Now, every day you see working people and visitors trying new restaurants.

It's not just downtown where you can get different cuisines. Now, every neighborhood in Toronto has a food plaza.

The list goes on with different restaurants.

Halal Food Market Trend

In the summer of 2024, it was reported in CTV News that many restaurants are going to provide halal chicken now.

Halal food has always been there in Ontario, but now many international fast food restaurants are bringing halal food options.

That is, if you go to a restaurant, you can request halal food. That is a new trend for many South Asian restaurants, which don't provide halal food.

I think that is because many Muslims are in Canada overall, and where I am in Ontario, the Muslim population is huge.

That is why there is a halal food market going on. As a halal consumer myself, I can say having halal food at every restaurant.

It gives you a homey feeling, but it also provides accessibility to others.

The halal food was the trend of the summer of 2024.

More and more halal restaurants.
Places like Ridgeway Plaza in Mississauga, which is a halal food market.

Other places besides Ridgeway, you can find a halal food market.

Was this the trend of the summer of 2024?

Yes, it was because more halal food restaurants .

More halal food festivals.

Some of Toronto's Halal Food Festivals are:

Halal Ribfest

Toronto Halal Food Festival

Taste of Middle East

Halal Food in Celebration Square

Halal Food Expo

These festivals are trending, and every time, there is something new.

Food Tourism Trends in 2025

These are my predictions on the food tourism trends in 2025:

1. More food influencers campaign
2. More restaurants opening
3. Different menus in each restaurant
4. A lot of global expansion for the restaurants, for example, Tim Hortons, Costa
5. More fried chicken restaurants
6. Vegan menu in many restaurants
7. Restaurants working towards charity; right now, it's really about Mcdonald's and Tim Hortons. More restaurants working on this cause.
8. Holiday menu to be developed at every restaurant
9. More discounts
10. More restaurants using Uber Eats

Social Media

For a food blogger, social media has a huge role.

That can be:

1. Promoting the stores
2. Promoting your food blog
3. Supporting businesses
4. Getting opportunities

These are some key facts about how social media is huge when it comes to food blogging.

In 2025 and 2026, food bloggers will use social media a lot.

Also, with new restaurants opening, that is why promoting restaurants on social media is important.

1. Promoting Stores

Often at stores, there are long weekend deals, or discounts, or a new menu at different restaurants.

These restaurants can be regular or take-out restaurants.

Restaurants are always promoting something new.

That is where food bloggers come in.

That is because food bloggers are often covering what is new at each restaurant. This can be throughout the year:

New Year's, Christmas, Family Day, or any other occasional day.

2. Promoting Your Food Blog

This is where the food blogger comes in. Promoting your food blogger. It's about engaging the community and engaging views.

Collaborating with different restaurants also means promoting your food blog. When you think of it, the restaurant promotes its food, and the food blogger reviews it.

3. Supporting Business

When you are doing a food review, you are also supporting a business. When it's a local brand or a food chain, that is how to support the business in the community. That is through local events and food reviews.

4. Getting Opportunities

When you get one opportunity with one restaurant, you get another restaurant, which will want to collaborate with you.

When you do your first restaurant review, you tag the company.

Eventually, restaurants will connect with you.

Keep doing food reviews and keep connecting.

Hashtags

When it comes to food tourism, hashtags are important.

That is because you have your own hashtag and get a following.

The hashtags I use are "Mississauga," "Brampton."

My own hashtag "HunyahTravelsBlog."

And sometimes, it will be the restaurant name, for example, "ChaiiwalaBrampton" or "DspotMalton."

These are a few to name.

This is a good technique to increase your social media presence as a food blogger.

About the Author

Hunyah is a content creator with a community development background .Hunyah is currently studying settlement counselling at Durham College. Also teaching adult education at Seneca College. Hunyah is a spoken word artist and content creator.

LinkedIn:
https://ca.linkedin.com/in/hunyah-irfan-blogger351

Instagram:
https://www.instagram.com/officalhunyahtravels/

Youtube:
https://www.youtube.com/@officalhunyahtravels1